PRAISE FOR
EACH KNUCKLE WITH SUGAR

"Sarah Levine's award-winning debut collection introduces us to Herman and Begonia, two people who embark on a love affair as they try to find a way out of a landscape stripped bare by loneliness and grief. There is a strangeness, an intensity, a blurring of the real and the surreal that makes this tale of love and loss intimate and authentic. Levine has a strong command of the image, metaphor, and simile, that renders these poems vivid and dreamlike. If there is grief, there is also humor: Herman's lists of questions to ask Begonia on their dates are original, to say the least. As they speak in turn, in their fragmented voices, Herman and Begonia become achingly human, their need for love and their thwarted attempts at salvation all too familiar."

—Martín Espada,
National Book Award Winner for *Floaters*

"*Each Knuckle with Sugar* is the poetry of rapture, a destabilizing state of transformation in which old garments are dropped, and all things are made new. The speakers of these persona poems, Herman and Begonia, testify to their bewilderment at having found one another and fallen into a ferocious love born in the disorienting wake of grief. This unexpected love, full of intelligence and awe, both rearranges the world while also giving each speaker a clarity of witness to the extraordinary wonder of being alive. Herman says, 'This is my truest story' in the opening poem, 'Brave' and we know that every word of this book is truth uttered between two lovers, become embodied in the bones of the reader. In the poem, 'Instant Hymn' Begonia says, 'and I want to/ wash my hands less pulling red/ birds out of each other/ All heart and dirt/ and everything would be new/ because there is newness in the best things.' As they speak, each to their beloved, they claim their own particular testimony of their separate stories, while weaving and stitching a new language between them, binding their lives together even in loss—through the enduring language of poetry itself. This book is incredible. I think of the poems from this collection all the time. There isn't anything in the manuscript I would change at all. It's just perfect. The language makes me want to write—right now!—you know that feeling? The best feeling when you read someone else's work and it fills you with energy to get up and write harder."

—Heathen (Heather Derr-Smith),
author of *Thrust*

"I have been reading Sarah Levine's poems for the past decade and in this luminous first collection she fulfills the promise of her earlier work. *Each Knuckle with Sugar* explores the romantic relationship between Herman and Begonia who meet at his mother's funeral. Each poem in which they inhabit is vivid, lyrical, poignant, often passionate and always intimate. As their relationship matures the metaphoric language is never predictable, a touch eccentric and always blissfully original. Read these poems and I guarantee you will bask in their humanity and, ultimately, be transformed in the mystery of their elegance."

—Kevin Pilkington,
author of *Playing Poker with Tennessee Williams*

"Open Sarah Levine's *Each Knuckle with Sugar* and join the journey of Herman and Begonia's love, born beside a funeral's 'goodbye box,' nurtured in old cars, fed by passionate 'kissing with mouthfuls of jam,' tested through fire, betrayal, and regret, as it rolls down 'bony roads scattered with elms and white churches.' Prepare to fall enthralled to the music of Levine's language, her magical surprises, the way she places realist images beside wild metaphors to make both burst alive, 'pulling red / birds out of each-other. / All heart and dirt.' Then when you've reached the end of the road, dancing 'like a bucket / rolling down a mountain,' whisper a thank you to Levine for bringing us along, slurp a little 'peach juice and rain,' and turn back to page one to take the ride again."

—Christopher Citro,
author of *If We Had a Lemon We'd Throw It* and *Call That the Sun*

"*Each Knuckle with Sugar* unravels and opens the reader. Through a multi-registered duet of ache, joy, longing, failings, and the search for meaningful human connection, Sarah Levine delivers an age-old story anew. A precise ear reveals image and language that startles and revives, a throat transforms into 'a hallway of snow,' giggling is reimagined into 'birds inside your body flap before hitting water,' and 'ears gust back like candles blown out by a child's untaught breath.' Levine fashions an ebb and flow between two personas within the liminality of arriving. Balancing the brutal, tender, playful, and spiraling, *Each Knuckle with Sugar* compels us toward an attunement of the spirit, to illuminate the unspoken, sought after wavelengths of connectedness we desire from a life lived."

—Anthony Cody,
author of *Borderland Apocrypha* and *The Rendering*

EACH KNUCKLE
WITH
SUGAR

Sarah Levine

Independently published by *Driftwood Press*
in the United States of America.

Managing Poetry Editor & Interviewer: Jerrod Schwarz
Poetry Editor: Sara Moore Wagner
Cover Image: Józef Simmler
Cover Design: Sally Franckowiak & Jerrod Schwarz
Interior Design: James McNulty
Copyeditor: Jerrod Schwarz & James McNulty
Fonts: Knockout, Merriweather, & Alternate Gothic Extra Condensed

Copyright © 2024 by Sarah Levine
All Rights Reserved.

No part of this publication
may be reproduced, stored in a retrieval
program, or transmitted, in any form or by
any means (electronic, mechanical,
photographic, recording, etc.), without
the publisher's written permission.

First published February 6th, 2024
ISBN-13: 978-1-949065-30-5

Please visit our website at www.driftwoodpress.com
or email us at editor@driftwoodpress.net.

CONTENTS

Foreword by Chen Chen   x

Brave   1

    I.   *jealous of the air between your knees*

Seeing Mother in her Goodbye Box   5
Newborn   6
With Begonia, After Mother's Funeral   7
Questions to Ask Begonia on our Second Date   8
Sleigh of Geese   9
Honk   10
Touch   11
Grief   12
Her Man   13
In the Rain   15
Drive   16
Instant Hymn   17

    II.   *summer lightning*

I Love the Way You Taste After Drinking Water   21
I Want   22
Tickle in the Throat   23
Questions to Ask Begonia on our Forty-Second Date   24
I Was a Cathedral   25
Bang-Bang   29
In the House of My Body Something Must Burn   31
Adultery   32

III.   *color of plums cut open too late*

Relationship Status 35
Sugar 36
I Hear a Goose in the Sky Say Again 37
Bag of Punches 38
Forgotten Things 39
Ripe Cotton 40
Knot 41
Therapy 42
A Horse is a Toy for Crazy People 43
Underwater Sky 44
Left 45

IV.   *rain is another four-letter word*

Dear Begonia 49
My Face is a Vase of Flowers Turning Toward the Sun 50

Interview: I Want to Break My Own Heart 53

FOREWORD
Chen Chen

Sarah Levine's *Each Knuckle with Sugar* enchants and engages by refusing to sound like anything less than the vertiginous thrill of love, the venomous throttle of heartbreak, and the verdant ache of falling even deeper for someone—and for the world you make, the world you are with that person. For instance:

> Is sky the most beautiful animal?
> Or snow?
> What about horses?
> How do you want your eggs tonight?
>
> —"Questions to Ask Begonia on our Forty-Second Date"

What wonderful, wonder-filled questions—the kind I wished a date would ask me, back when I was single in a major city and dating around and feeling, well, not very much. These questions are full of feeling; they spill over with ecstatic feeling and with wanting to feel ecstatically more. They're akin to a game my partner and I play, where one of us asks the other what would happen if, for example, "I turned into a giant spider with the face of that actor we hate? (Everything else about me is the same.)" The follow-up question's always, "Would you still love me?" The answer's always "yes" but maybe not "yes!" or "YES." There isn't always an embrace of the transformation (though surprises happen), but there's usually laughter. Sometimes, a groan that's really the rhetorical question, "Are you kidding me?" Sure, I'm kidding you, but play along, play with me, see what else happens if we follow these words and images further down (or up?) their weird path—that's at the heart of the game. The heart/ending of this Sarah Levine poem reminds me of the heart/ending of a Frank O'Hara poem, "For Grace, After a Party":

> [...] And someone you love enters the room
> and says wouldn't
>   you like the eggs a little
>
> different today?

Yes (YES), I'm saying the eggs are the heart of both of these poems and not just because eggs are where (how?) both poems end. Levine's "How do you want your eggs tonight" sort of answers O'Hara's "wouldn't / you like the eggs a little / different today?" by implying that the typical breakfast item will be enjoyed at night. That's a key difference. Levine's work offers an abundance of key differences. I say this mainly because, as a queer writer/reader who largely prefers love stories, love poems from a queer perspective, this book has me completely riveted—by a cis het romance! My tone may seem somewhat flippant, but seriously, that is no easy feat.

This book is not your run-of-the-mill straight romcom where "fate" (a.k.a. the gender binary) dictates the characters' every move, meeting, every moment of dialogue. The voices here—of Herman and Begonia—pulse with idiosyncrasy, swerve with passion, and ooze with questions. Theirs are restless voices, restlessly searching for music and feeling, freedom and meaning, individually as well as together.

As Begonia sings in "I Love the Way You Taste After Drinking Water":

> The trees think I am a giant flame and they
> are so afraid, summoning wind to toss me down the road and a road's job
> is to carry someone away. What do you think about when you see the moon
> during the day?

And Herman sings back in "Underwater Sky":

> In day when I see the moon I think of you, I think about
> what you are thinking about when you see the moon—a polar bear
> holding up the sky. No. *The stars hold up the sky*, is what mother used to say
> in her wool gloves and dress and I knew she was alive
> when I could hear her boat heart swung in sea.

Herman's grief for his mother is as central to this book as his love for Begonia. Begonia's relationship to trees—and fields and geese and her brother "built from geometry and Tuesday afternoon / rain"—is as crucial to this book as her relationship to the boy "whose voice makes flowers stand straighter in the sun" ("Drive"). These two are multidimensional, dizzyingly messy people with their quirks as well as their flaws. And it is equally their quirks that are or that become sources of conflict between one another and within themselves.

This is another key difference: in your typical straight (or frankly, also gay) romantic narrative, it's the flaws that are either overcome (happily ever after) or succumbed to (tragically). Either way, what matters is that the plot of *will they end up together* gets a firm resolution. But in these pages—and without giving away too much of this book's surprising, astonishing conclusion—it's the characters' quirks, really their strengths rather than their flaws, that are the focus, and ultimately it's Herman and Begonia's whole rich world of personalities and histories, their wild observations and wilder turns of phrase, that last. Long after the last page. This book is not so much a tale of *will they end up together* as a song of *whatever happens next, it will be glorious, because look at these two, listen to them sing on.*

After all, "[a] relationship is about inventing your own language," as French director Céline Sciamma put it in an interview. Sciamma directed the 2019 period drama, *Portrait of a Lady on Fire*, which features two women falling in love in 18th century France. In my 21st century American life I've gotten used to the fact that queer people often have to invent a language—outside of heteronormativity—to talk about the kinds of relationships, the kinds of love, that we experience. Such inventing arises from necessity. But should I feel used to it? What if it's not always from necessity? What if I continue to invent because I want to? Because I'm in love? Because I'm thinking about and desiring further love? Maybe it's time for a rewatch of Sciamma's beautiful film. I reference it here because Levine's work understands Sciamma's notion of shared invention so well, so freshly and tenderly.

As Herman sings in "Bang-Bang":

> And I know one day you will leave me like mother.
>
> I will stand over another goodbye box
> the geese will rage beside the moon.
> The books will grow inside the trees
>
> and I will kneel close enough
> to pick the hair from your chin.
> Not yet.
>
> Not today because your pockets are filled with peanuts.
> You are making a jelly sandwich and spilling laughter
> into my throat—

And Begonia sings back in "Sugar":

> Come home
>
> and kiss me until
> we become a gash

of sunlight, lift my dress
press your cheek

to my belly and kneel
without a word

waiting for my body
to become a wet gorgeous
star.

I love this book. I am so glad to be welcoming it into the world, into your hands. Look, some of its tanginess may leap off the page and startle your fingers. Some of its honey may stick to your knuckles. Let it.

Chen Chen
Rochester, NY

For Rose (1932–2010)
For Tony (1929–2012)

Brave

I was a little suit on a little boy, watching mother in her goodbye box. This is my truest story. Begonia's voice turned white in the sky and the cheat grass stung our toes. My face almost quiet. Your hands found my hands and your mouth found my mouth until my throat became a hallway of snow.

--

I.
jealous of the air between your knees

Seeing Mother in her Goodbye Box

It's easier to think of her cheeks pressed to a field
covered in white blossoms. The same field

that once held the footsteps of two dozen rabbits dusted in snow
or the turning carnival wheels last summer.

I want to watch the elephant's ears become aprons
in wind. When it got so hot everything

tasted like libraries dripping in gasoline. After the carnival she stood inside river
finding fish to scrub into diamonds while I pet the spine of her laughter.

The rest of the summer I spent too much time
with hands covering all the holes

that couldn't quit leaking from my face.
Now I cover myself in river

pray each scratch of sun will bruise enough color into my chest
to remind mirrors how the living look.

Newborn

Every time you kiss a boy
you are really kissing
another person's son
I think in the graveyard
finding your mouth
with my mouth,
a thicket of honeysuckle
our kiss newborn.
And other boys
play baseball and girls lean back
on the hoods of their cars
fixing picnic
until sandwiches only taste
like other peoples' hands.
And I want to call you
on the telephone every night
tell stories about fields trampled
by lonely circus animals.
One story about a skinny child
lifting his head to admire a rabbit
and its quiver
caught in the mouth
of the three-legged dog.

With Begonia, After Mother's Funeral

I lie in the field
when the stars turn on

and fire tells the wood
what to say.

There is melon in a bucket
spit the seeds out for planting

and I want a bicycle.
A seat and wheels

to ride to the river until
I smell mother's ghost asleep

in someone's garden.
And the neighbors never tell

when we steal begonia blossoms
to place behind each other's ears and run

through other peoples' backyards. Even this one time
when the rains begin and begin until our skin

becomes wet paper, and when spoken
the three syllables of your first name sing papercut.

Questions to Ask Begonia on our Second Date

Any pets?

Does your pet like you?

Has your pet ever seen you naked?

Where have you stood all night listening to rain?

Could we ride cross county, in a canoe?

With life jackets the color of cherry life savers?

Is your skin always the color of egg whites?

Do you ever wish you were made of bark?

Or clay or milk or light?

Could you wear more dresses with pockets?

Zippers or buttons?

Did you keep the bumper car tokens?

Are they in your pocket?

What is the cruelest thing you have ever done?

When you cry, are you difficult to hold?

Who performed your first haircut?

Is it someone's mother?

Can you juggle wind battered apples?

Will I see you tomorrow?

Sleigh of Geese

I tell you if I could do anything
I would grow the longest arms
to scratch the moon because the moon
is my favorite mosquito bite.

You just stand and chew stand and chew
and suddenly wish I had a sleigh of geese
to nip my ankles pink and make
the ground smell of half bitten apples.

Our geese
would huddle together like eggs in a carton,
lazy and watching
you tell me about the people we will grow into.

Your breath on my neck like a music
raising my arms into the air
like two skinny kites
searching for a gallop of wind.

Honk

When the geese fly over my head
I think about being young together.

Hold hands everywhere we go.
Sit in the car with the windows down

honking for rain. When you kiss my nose
I feel charming like a strawberry admired by its farmer.

You light matches and blow them out
so the car smells like a birthday party.

And I lick your finger
the way I used to lick icing off a candle.

I make a fist to remember the size of my own heart
and punch you in the chest to pass the yearbook.

Instead of reading we just look at the words inside
until I start to wonder if your old girlfriend

ever looked at you like this and thought
here's someone who will watch the sky stay put with me.

And then I lift my favorite
white dress over my shoulders and wipe my forehead

wipe the wheel, wipe the windshield and book
trying to make everything new again.

Touch

You try to hold my hand
but I just want to hold
your pocket.

You have this crooked jaw
that likes to say son
of a gun.

When you giggle
birds inside your body
flap before hitting water.

I am afraid of drinking
too much water Begonia Jackson
I am uneasy with scissors until put in my pocket.

We could have
the longest babies
name them sons and after guns.

Grief

I saw mother say goodbye to her own mother
sitting on church steps, leaking all over her starchy dress and gloves

and I wanted to shake her head open to turn off the water.
When I say goodbye to mother

I know the box holds an imposter
and I fill with the sweetest madness to bark at the moon to scare the stars away.

She liked to go missing—
Through the trees with her shoes in her hands

and I would find her asleep in someone's garden—
Filled her pockets with matches so she could carry on and burn.

This summer, the farm animals flee
leaving a path through trampled wheat

and I spend too many nights
beneath a cloak of sky

pull the darkness close, pluck stars
off invisible thorns. Expose the soft parts of each arm

to the moon. For some reason, this reminds me of my uncle's son
when he mistook shovels for long necked birds, pointed to the dirtiest one

perched against a wall in his father's shed, and asked us, this half-circle of men,
In the dark, won't he be lonely, won't he be cold?

Her Man

I am a terrible swimmer
All elbows and lungs.

But you—
Forearms swifter

Than slide trombones
Are song

Sweet-boned
Begonia—

Wet yellow braid
Caught in wind.

I know your noise
Belly full of fish.

I feel sorry for my shirts.
Mother sewed my name into each one

On the tag
Herman Herman Her Man.

Could I be?
Could I sew my name into your pocket?

Let my fingers brood and gasp.
I am jealous of the air between your knees

The dropped stitch on your hem.
The geese squawk

And you turn toward them and their bugle throats
Mesmerized by the unrehearsed choir of wings.

I will pluck geese from the sky
Knock-kneed in fields of mint and pepper,

In rain when bones become spoons—
A throb song.

When the wings are quiet and smell of blown out candles
And you will kneel, feet bare

A wet prayer folding from your lips.
Let my lips

Listen into the shell of your ear—
Bony roads scattered with elms and white churches.

In the Rain

You set your shoes free while your hair turned itself into wool and your dress became thin and your eyelashes became bristles and you held my hand and I asked my hand what to do I asked the clouds and seeds and shovel and you hung your dress on a stalk of wheat and I stopped asking

Drive

We watch the wind ruin a wheat field's face
head lights willing a deer to stop and stand stupid
breathe stupid die stupid. We keep driving. We keep the windows open

the radio singing about storm the mosquitoes singing about blood
at stops signs I let them suck. When I was a child all I wanted
was to turn good turn sweet like pancake on griddle, chop all

my hair and leave it to rest in brother's shoe. I loved my brother, and he loved my hair
color of burning bush and name me one girl who has never hidden
from a boy whose voice makes flowers stand straighter in the sun.

Herman has loud teeth, an appetite for rivers. Water will not make me beautiful.
Don't you know that? Don't you know the river in June
is too tall to enter and the flowers are too young to pick.

Who does the sky belong to anyway? I ask my brother, teeth dotted with blackberry seeds.
He kneels beside his river and looks at the sky and the sky looks right back at him
and he will put his lips inside the shell of my ear and shout

no one.

Instant Hymn

I feel like straw
in the scarecrow.

When I am with you
I feel like straw

in the scarecrow in the rain
in the mud

when dogs
chew each-other's ears

and storm
makes the grass grow.

I should touch the back
of your neck more.

Dance like a bucket
rolling down a mountain.

In the dark
in the driveway

we stare at the moon
pick fruit off a tree

and I want to
wash my hands less pulling red

birds out of each-other.
All heart and dirt

and everything would be new
because there is newness in the best things.

II.
summer lightning

I Love the Way You Taste After Drinking Water

I was taught to kneel in a night gown
gathering stars spilled from my brother's hands.

Brother built from geometry and Tuesday afternoon rain.
Sometimes, I lie in bed clutching my own hair, dark river

hung by two clothespins and I want to kiss someone, our mouths
collapsing under the weight of honey

to smell of pussy willow and love for no reason.
I met you on a road in a town

where men knock their knuckles
against a hound dog's head and trees wave

when I walk because I am wearing the reddest dress
I own. The trees think I am a giant flame and they

are so afraid, summoning wind to toss me down the road and a road's job
is to carry someone away. What do you think about when you see the moon

during the day? Do you think about your childhood and how much of it ended
when you learned what was really up there.

I Want

To become mutt with a paw's
quick stitch in the sand
longing to hold a fish.
To lick each gills
flutter, invent song
made from instrument
of tongue and bite.
Send me out into
this world to outrun
a flock of rain knees
knocking so fast
my ears gust
back like candles
blown out by a child's
untaught breath.
I drink from garden hose
chase tricycles
into traffic and some minutes
even hear my heart kick
like a can tossed
into a field full of goats.
Seeds
knock through my fur
and I am in love with you
standing tip toe
selling corn
down the road.
You sweat sugar until mosquitoes turn drunk.
You smell too ripe
too alive to be left alone.

Tickle in the Throat

I hate weather moving through your lungs and I hate my lungs
two bloody engines scaring birds back into the branches

I hate the way you stand there watching me thrash like blade against field
and I want to hurt you

I want to steal sky in your mouth I want
to set a match inside your ear and watch your face bloom

Questions to Ask Begonia on our Forty-Second Date

What is the first lie you ever told?

Why does your laughter remind me of children running out of their shoes?

If someone were chasing you, would you keep running or stop and fight?

When walking through the devil's throat, which weapon do you want by your side?

Do you prefer clapping or the silence in between claps?

Will you yank weeds until your arms become wet, kneeling blades?

Can you change the lightbulb at the top of the stairs?

Could you teach me the definition of petrichor after you kiss me in the middle of allergy season?

Is sky the most beautiful animal?

Or snow?

What about horses?

How do you want your eggs tonight?

I Was a Cathedral

l: For S

Last April, he drew flowers across my collarbone,
and the blossoms looked like damp, uneven feathers

until he smudged them into one thick thunderbolt.
My brother met him in biology,

lab partners. He hid swollen frogs in his pockets, later
scrubbed his own hands into bloodstained flowers.

My enemy is this skin suit I zip, these
sour knuckles, fists as fat as doorknobs of homes we broke into.

I thought love was kissing with mouthfuls of jam
smearing vowels across each-other's chests, screaming so my lungs

church into train stations
filled with trash and footsteps and sun.

ll: For M

Too much oxygen planted in the cemetery grass
to force the living to keep breathing, each lung

a beehive, refusing to retire.
Maybe it was walking in grass above

so many bodies, bodies that lived loud, strange lives
thrust in overripe cities or caught

in a snaggle of limbs.
Isn't love just an antidote to death?

I said to no one in particular, not the boy

walking two steps behind me or the white birds
pecking at our elongated shadows

and I rolled my eyes because I knew he would kiss me
and when he did everything tasted of lemon rind.

lll: For R

He touched my cheek
and I wanted to cut off his hand

IV: Dear Herman

The church is hive
all sermon, air fanned

from idle bodies' breath
and in my seat, I think

what would happen if you died.
If I stepped out of church

clutching your photo
later used to blot blood from tablecloth

inside brother's overgrown tool shed
beside the ladder and open paint can color of spun

honey, dress damp with the stench of summer
heart louder than dynamite stick thrown to the fish

and sometimes
you make it difficult to live.

Bang-Bang

She makes my tongue dumb
and when I lick her knees
I taste the heads of hammers.

I saw her first in mother's car
when she stepped through the street
in only the arms of a sweater.

I wanted to jump off my school desk and wrestle a thrush into her throat.

When I saw her third at mother's funeral
she put her hand inside my pocket
smiled with teeth bigger than light bulbs.

And I felt clean like someone just shucked me into the world.
I have a girl—
I have the girl who meets me under the trees

and lets me look close enough to see the hair on her chin.
When I look, I get hungry
and I realize I know nothing,

so I sock stalks of corn in the face.
I roll in puddles and plead for summer lightning to lift me off my feet
for I love you.

My hands and teeth and bloody pulp of a heart
love you.
And I know one day you will leave me like mother.

I will stand over another goodbye box
the geese will rage beside the moon.
The books will grow inside the trees

and I will kneel close enough
to pick the hair from your chin.
Not yet.

Not today because your pockets are filled with peanuts.
You are making a jelly sandwich and spilling laughter
into my throat—

Filling me the way a dozen thrushes fill a chimney.

In the House of My Body Something Must Burn

Heart kick the windows out
and ride your unicycle

through this
body's skinny streets.

Heart be good
be a red tablecloth

covered in glass pitchers of cream and
strawberry jam jars, loaves

of brown bread cooling underneath
the sycamore's outstretched shade.

When the grocer's son
knocks twice

on the door of your grandmother's trailer
and when he bites

your cold lip, heart
be a pack of dogs

trying to outrun
squawks of the hen house
set on fire.

Adultery

Before the clouds brewed into storm
And the geese squawked into smoke
I stood watching his teeth
Unzip you free from dress
Inside your grandmother's trailer
And I became a trampled field
With too many farm tools
And a dog that pouts
Beneath the corn stalks shade
Trying to hide from a herd of flies

III.
color of plums cut open too late

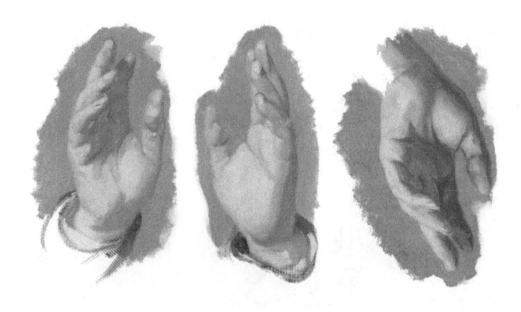

Relationship Status

And if I told the entire story
I would never get it back

Sugar

Do you remember
when I stole

your suspenders.
Bit the backs

of your hands
when you touched

a piano note wrong,
nursed each knuckle

with sugar, whistled
lullaby into your ear

until you forgave me.
Come home

and kiss me until
we become a gash

of sunlight, lift my dress
press your cheek

to my belly and kneel
without a word

waiting for my body
to become a wet gorgeous
star.

I Hear a Goose in the Sky Say Again

You are one loud sentence
someone finds wherever there is dancing.

These days I leave parties alone
on the walk home taste

the time we talked about toys geese and love,
when I wore all white in the grass.

The things we do in the dark do us good
you said before your hand

fell from the back of my neck.
It was forever ago, me with a body

full of mad flapping birds.
You loved to watch

a storm of geese
flock into our field

while I knelt in bent wheat, stared at my hands.

Bag of Punches

By day I break glass and roll tires.
In this two-bite town, the boys grow into men and the men grow back into campfire.

Take my money to the campgrounds
throw bread to the birds and wait for their stomachs to explode.

Can't drive past a wheat field without heart becoming bumper car
punching through a mountain.

By night, I sit on hoods of cars with hands that rise up and take--
names, wind, and bruises the color of plums cut open too late.

It feels good to be underestimated, to emerge from a cage
after wrestling the moon, sit on the edge of someone's swimming pool,

and listen to a neighbor's daughter talk triumph in a body so beautiful it makes me wince.
I loved someone and you were just footsteps: one punch, two kicks, three kisses.

You were born with a name only thunder could pronounce.

Forgotten Things

Imagine you put your face against store windows
selling paper flowers and wooden horses.
You were made because two bodies forgot
risk, ignored recitation of kiss kiss tremble, a sermon
announcing the end of free love.
Love taught you to stand inside an ocean, feel the fish
smear their scales on wave after wave.

Love taught no manners
fire set to someone's orchard so you become peach jam for days. How absurd
to be given a mouth that craves fruit bruised into sugar.
How easy it is now for you to chase chickens
wearing the reddest dress, legs running loud like forgotten pianos
being banged into existence.

Ripe Cotton

And this tiny white dress is alive-

this crop of sick cotton
grown just above the knee
for the dog to lick in between
chasing chickens into flight.

We used to chase chickens
barefoot and brutal carving
our voices into locomotives
hungry for a bird's feather ruffled-

inventing sound so ripe
the dog could not help

but bite the air.

Knot

I stuffed your hair
in my jacket pocket.

Stroked its feathers and told stories
about a snorting dark horse

the birds watch and flies heckle.
I still get the knots telling me about

how this body can hurt.
How easy

to be alone and forget
how to not be alone.

All I can do is walk to the river,
walk into wetness.

Until my hands depend on the cold
fish to run through them.

Until my body turns
into a stone flung deeper.

Until my lungs, arms, and legs
can no longer be quiet
and start to play.

Therapy

The only way to quiet my hands
is to submerge them in a bucket of ice.

I painted the bedroom blue
to keep an ocean between us.

In this dream
I glue broken glass

into boat, the bedroom walls
collapse into cold water.

I wake coughing salt and shudder.
In the dark, brother's voice

pecks my blood
like a white beaked bird.

Are you thinking of hurting yourself?
Yes. Anyone who answers differently is a liar.

I am tired of swallowing handfuls of apple seeds
waiting for my body to become a tree drenched in sunlight

waiting for storm to clatter all my branches into symphony.

A Horse is a Toy for Crazy People

Do you remember running out of your shoes to find
me in the field, to whisper into my open mouth:

Your knees are baby rabbits I forgot to kiss.
Now my knees are skinny horses

stomping through wheat
stomping through cold water.

A horse is a toy for crazy people
you said once, a long time ago

when we climbed the tallest tree
to watch the birds burst into stars.

Let's be ourselves
because I am tired of taking people

I do not love to the movies.
Two boys kissed me

in brother's overgrown tool shed
because they grew bored

picking wings from the cricket's back.
Too many of us stay where we are made

and I am tired of waiting
for you to hang my favorite

white dress on a stalk of wheat
with a note that reads

Take Me Home.

Underwater Sky

In day when I see the moon I think of you, I think about
what you are thinking about when you see the moon— a polar bear
holding up the sky. No. *The stars hold up the sky,* is what mother used to say
in her wool gloves and dress and I knew she was alive
when I could hear her boat heart swung in sea.

I still want to see the ocean. How big it really is, underwater sky
with shark and seahorse and shell.
I miss you and your hands. If you asked them to touch me
they wouldn't recognize my face anymore.
I wish I still knew mother, but she was carried out of church, marched
into the field where the cows kneel before rain. You are gone too-

Left

You left my sheet in sweat
        The scent of a raccoon guarding her baby

Left the shadows of mulberry and mackerel
        How water feels without its town of fish

Left boats painted yellow and alligators with pimples on their cheeks
        Before I could dress myself in envelopes and stamp

Left sunflowers and cracked corn
        When the wind takes everything in its fists and blows the world blind

IV.
rain is another four-letter word

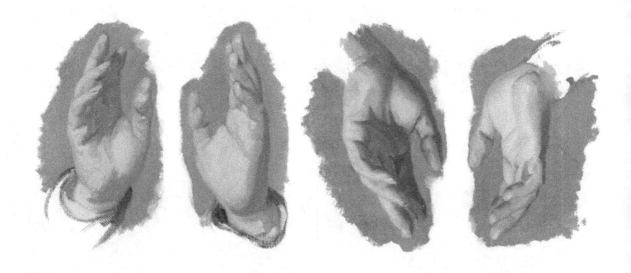

Dear Begonia

Close your eyes. Open your mouth. Choke
on this flood of sunlight. I will wait beside river
build a cage out of broken bones, dab kerosene
on each knuckle, pull fistfuls
of yellow flowers until gold
drips down each lifted arm.
Don't be stupid enough to try to kill
the fox in your blood. I turn coyote beneath moon
wake up in clover clotted field and I cannot
decode each vowel of silence each welt of blood lust.
You left me for Massachusetts, word with a long forehead.

Tell me about the ocean

I know you hear the waves break like snorting Clydesdales.
I know I am coward, bruise petals against my chest
lie on the floors of other peoples' bedrooms and weep.
A body is only a box of breaths even cowards
are built from boxes of breath. When trucks
from the nearby highway drive too quickly
the bedroom walls shake, and you once pressed your mouth
against the parts of my shadow I loathed called my arms
backyard riots. We said goodbye on different doorsteps
licked salt from the backs of each-others' necks
walked home thirsty. I am still thirsty
leaving orchards with unpaid peaches and fingertips
dusted in cobweb. I slurp peach juice and rain, watch
couples on street corners touch the rooms of each-others' bodies.
Is field still your favorite room?
Do you still throw paper napkins into the sky
pretending they are birds? Tonight,
I sleep at the bottom of an empty swimming pool
until thirst revisits me, and all I can do
is hunch in the darkness sip your ghost
from my cupped hands and wait.

My Face is a Vase of Flowers Turning Toward the Sun

I always knew dead was a four-letter word
same family as fear

or envy's mouth folding into a switch blade
beheading the neighbor's peonies.

Rain is another four-letter word
responsible for babies, for

nearby gardens to look just born
and screaming.

Do you remember, we went swimming in the rain after painting the shed?
You were dripping color into the grass until river

draped over each of our knuckles' tiny boulders
and both our mothers will be dead one day.

That four-letter word again
its fingerprints on the buttons of each blue sweater hanging in mother's closet.

Just because my mother is still alive
does not mean I have never known grief

you once said, facing the sun
and I felt the sky crack inside each knuckle.

I am tired of always apologizing
because trying to explain how shame

doesn't seek permission to ransack a body
feels selfish.

I should spend more time with my face
watching the geese turn their backs on this neighborhood leaving

only the sky to miss you.

I WANT TO BREAK MY OWN HEART
A Conversation between Sarah Levine and Jerrod Schwarz

Let me start by saying how happy we are to be publishing *Each Knuckle with Sugar*! This is an astounding collection of poems, and I cannot wait to dive into the craft and inspiration behind the work. I want to start off with one of the book's larger concerns and themes: the body. What are the challenges and joys when writing about the human body? Was there any presiding goal you had when you set out to write these poems?

Thank you so much, Jerrod. The fractured body is an essential element in *Each Knuckle with Sugar*. Herman is specifically obsessed with mouths and knees. Mouths remind me of so many things: movie theaters, wallets, playgrounds. They are beautiful yet barbaric. The mouth is responsible for facilitating speech and intimacy. Knees to me are a symbol of innocence. Do you remember the first time you skinned your knee? The body is a collage of accumulated personal history (scars, trauma, memories); the body is a flag we wave throughout the performance of our lives. What matters most to me in every poem is language. The heat (Thanks, Shira!) and prosody, the physical joy of words cannonballing off a tongue's dive board. Sound gushing through a body's interior hallways. For each utterance to be authentic, concrete, and alive. The music of it all.

On a craft level, one of my favorite aspects of this collection is your use of disparate line lengths. There are poems with short lines, poems with long lines, and poems with a mix. I would love to know what the first drafts of these poems look like. What visual changes do your poems go through from first draft to last?

This collection began over a decade ago with poems only in one form: prose blocks. A paragraph length of prose chronicling a Herman misadventure. Begonia had not discovered her voice yet. These misadventures included Herman watching a man sob by the riverbank, Herman gazing at himself in the reflection of a nearby car window, Herman taking Begonia to the movies, etc. In Patrick Rosal's grad workshop I wrote a list poem entitled "Why Begonia Left" and in conference Pat encouraged me to experiment with new forms maybe epistolary or villanelle, to play around with the architecture of the page, to use each stanza, each line break, each piece of punctuation as instruments to ultimately create a working song. As the years passed, I started to think about how poems can dialogue with each other through structure or language or voice, how a manuscript is really the construction of a tightly wound symphony. Now, my go-to first draft form is dumping everything into a notebook. When the inspiration strikes, I just write unabashedly, resisting each kernel of self-doubt and fear. After reading the initial word flood out loud I start to assemble line breaks, stanzas, and punctuation... always guided by language, listening to where I naturally breathe. Each poem is its own animal. Is the imagery clean and concrete? Vivid, surprising verbs? Does the poem have a heartbeat? What's the weather here? Some poems are done in five minutes while others I interrogate for years.

I really love that goal, of creating a "working song" out of your poems, because it speaks to poetry as inherently structural, maybe even sculptural. When writing (or revising) what are your *visual* goals with a poem? Perhaps more specifically, what do you want readers to notice about the shape of a poem even before they read it?

That's such a wonderful question. I think each reader should investigate how a poem is made to deduce greater meaning. There is power in the actual composition of a page. How many spaces are between words or stanzas? Enjambment? How does the visual representation of each poem facilitate breath? Reading a poem out loud is physical, tactile, there is beauty in the way words are strung and splattered. I gave an earlier draft of the book to my friend and poet Christopher Citro to read and told him concerns I had regarding the development of Begonia's voice. He recommended writing poems in Begonia's voice on the right side of the page and only using the left for Herman poems. This was a game changer. It changed the alchemy of the Herman/Begonia relationship. There is a visual component now embodying the ebb and flow of their courtship; their story feels even more intimate.

Love, both familial and romantic, seems to be one of the book's main concerns. As an editor, it almost feels revelatory to read a collection about love in 2023 that doesn't rely on cliché or tired, romantic tropes. Did this theme appear organically as you were writing or was it a guiding intention from the outset?

That means the world to me. Thank you! The collection swerved in a new direction after the loss of my maternal grandparents within two years. My grandparents helped raise me and were an integral part of my childhood and home. I had never experienced grief like that before, and without sounding too sentimental, this period of time radically changed me. Writing became and still is a lifeline. I think every poem I write is a love poem. Every poem I write is an opportunity to reconnect with the dead (including former versions of myself), to say things I was not brave enough to say.

In keeping with this theme of reconnection, can you tell me your thoughts on how poems investigate the past? This might not be a very comprehensive observation, but it seems like a lot of poetry that investigates, as you say, "former versions" of

ourselves gets corralled into the wide pen of confessional poetry. In poems that you've written about the past, what are you most interested in unearthing?

A memory or shard of truth. Survival. I want to break my own heart. I want to wrestle grief in the mud during a thunderstorm then sip tea beside my grief on the back porch steps. I want to remember I have knuckles and lungs and blood that sloshes from one artery to another. I never want to forget this silent awe that drapes over my shoulders when I crouch on the floor of my closet trying to write yet another poem, trying to converse with a place I moved away from or a person who left me too soon.

What authors, poets, artists or other creatives inspired these poems?

Thank you to my original teachers, the texts that informed and inspired Herman and Begonia's world: *Crush* by Richard Siken, *Night Sky with Exit Wounds* by Ocean Vuong, *Sum of Every Lost Ship* by Allison Titus, *The Lifting Dress* by Lauren Berry, *Autobiography of Red* by Anne Carson, *Kingdom Animalia* by Aracelis Girmay, *The Book of Whispering in the Projection Booth* by Joshua Marie Wilkinson, *Scratching the Ghost* by Dexter L. Booth, *The Great Fires* by Jack Gilbert, *Bright Brave Phenomena* by Amanda Nadelberg, *The Battlefield Where the Moon Says I Love You* by Frank Stanford, *Book of Questions* by Pablo Neruda and translated by William O'Daly.

What are you working on next? Do you ever plan to return to these personas for future work?

A new school year just started! I teach seventh grade English and twelfth grade AP LIT in Massachusetts. During this school year my primary focus is teaching, completing the *Teachers for Global Classrooms* Fulbright fellowship, and my students. My students give me so much hope and joy. I'm deliriously proud of them. During time off, a few projects call my name: cultivating a creative writing textbook for middle and high school students and wrangling Herman and Begonia into a novel. I feel best when I read and write poems. Poems force me to pay attention. Reading induces necessary pauses. (Thanks, Aysha for this amazing phrase!).

At *Driftwood*, we often get inquiries from poets asking for advice on how to write, compile, and publish a full-length collection of poetry. What advice was helpful when you were at the beginning stages? What do you wish you had been told earlier?

Surprise yourself. Be patient. Take risks. Get lost. Trust the process. Trust the inner music your words make. You will find your way through the forest.

NOTES

"Sleep at the bottom of an empty swimming pool" borrowed from "How I Became Fatherless" by K-Ming Chang.

"Covering all the holes that couldn't quit leaking" borrowed from Melissa Broder.

"When you cry are you difficult to hold?" borrowed and altered from *The Man Suit* by Zachary Schomburg.

The following lines are borrowed from Amanda Nadelberg's collection *Bright Brave Phenomena*: "Hot tempered story;" "It was forever ago;" "Darkness does us good;" We do things in the dark;" "One loud sentence."

"Horse is a toy for crazy people" spoken by Sam Virzi during a drive.

"Relationship Status" inspired by the Federico Garcia Lorca quote: "If I told you the whole story it would never end…"

"Affair" is inspired by Jim Harrison's *Letters to Yesenin*.

Part of the title: "Goose Says Again in the Sky" from Quin spoken during read-aloud in our second-grade classroom with magical Mrs. Jones in 2014.

"My mouth blooms like a cut" is the first line from Anne Sexton's "The Kiss."

ACKNOWLEDGEMENTS

My gratitude to the editors and readers of the following journals in which versions of these poems first appeared:

"Forgotten Things," *The Paris-American*, 2020
"I Hear a Goose Say Again in the Sky," First Runner Up, Federico Garcia Lorca Poetry Prize, *Green Briar Review*, 2017
"In the House of My Body Something Must Burn," *Bodega*, 2015
"Bag of Punches," *Passages North*, 2019
"I Want," *Whiskey Island*, 2014
"Ripe Cotton," *Fourteen Hills*, 2014
"A Horse is a Toy for Crazy People," *Green Mountains Review*, 2013
"My Face is a Vase of Flowers Turning Toward the Sun" is an excerpt from "Birds Are Loosely Folded Napkins Thrown into the Sky," *Best New Poets Anthology*, 2013
"Sleigh of Geese," Poem of the Moment: Masspoetry.org, 2013
"Knot," *Green Mountains Review Online*, 2013
"Hunting," "Sleigh of Geese" *PANK*, 2013
"Drive," *Vinyl*, 2013
"Bang-Bang," Winner of *Westchester Review* Writers' Under 30 Poetry Contest and MVICW Creative Writing Award, 2012
"Touch," *Westchester Review*, 2012
"Her Man," *Elimae*, 2011
"Honk," *Handsome*, 2014
"Dear Begonia," a finalist in *River Heron Review* Editor's Prize, 2022
"Instant Hymn," *Driftwood Press 2023 Anthology*, 2023

Versions of some of these pieces appeared in the chapbook *Her Man* (The New Megaphone Press, 2014) and the chapbook *Take Me Home* (Finishing Line Press, 2020).

THANKS

Thank you: *Driftwood Press*! Jerrod, James, and the whole team for your encouragement and vision and excitement from day one.

Thank you: Martín Espada, Heathen (Heather Derr-Smith), Kevin Pilkington, Anthony Cody, and Christopher Citro for writing the most generous, big-hearted blurbs and taking the time to be on this journey with me. I would not be the writer or person I am today without each of you. Thank you for mentoring me, for seeing me.

Thank you: Chen Chen for dressing Herman and Begonia up in the most beautiful foreword I could possibly imagine. Thank you for poetry dates and over a decade of friendship. Thank you for reading a draft of the manuscript, circling the line "Each Knuckle with Sugar" and stating, "Here's your title." You were right. You are always right.

Thank you to the institutions that gave me space and time and community: University of Massachusetts Amherst, Juniper Summer Writing Institute, Sarah Lawrence College, Smith College, Noepe Literary Arts Center, Wellspring House, Martha's Vineyard Institute for Creative Writing, *Kenyon Review* Online Writers Workshop (I miss our cohort!), *Tin House* Online Writers Workshop, National Endowment for the Humanities Institute, Pioneer Valley Chinese Immersion Charter School, and Williston Northampton School.

Thank you to the teachers, mentors, and writers who have helped me in more ways than they will ever know: Diane Tetreault, Suzanne Gardinier (and our first-year seminar cohort), Marina Jones, Justin Ahren, Patrick Rosal, Betsy Wheeler, Frank Bidart, Jonathan Escoffery.

Thank you to my students, friends, and family who galvanize me every day. Special shout outs to Catherine Mikkelsen and Dialynn Dwyer for being there through it all. Elizabeth Mikesch for reading an early draft and giving such thoughtful notes, Chris Ayala for capturing the moments, and to Julia Glenn, reading at your wedding is one of the greatest joys of my entire life. That version of "Sleigh of Geese" is forever yours and Richie's.

Thank you to my parents: For your steadfast belief and love.

Lastly, thank you Sam and Fat Boy for gifting me my favorite sounds: When I open the door each night and Sam's voice bounces from the kitchen while Fat Boy's tail thumps against the living room floor, I know I am home.

Sarah Levine is a Pushcart Prize nominee and author of two chapbooks, *Take Me Home*, a finalist for the New Women's Voices Chapbook Competition (*Finishing Line Press*, 2020) and *Her Man* (*New Megaphone Press*, 2014). Her work has appeared in *Passages North*, Best New Poets anthology, *Green Mountains Review*, and *The Paris American* among other publications. She earned her MFA from Sarah Lawrence College, MAT from Smith College, and BA from UMASS Amherst Honors College. Levine is a 2023-2024 Teachers for Global Classrooms Fulbright fellow and teaches 7th Grade ELA and 12th Grade AP Literature at Williston Northampton School where she currently holds the Richard C. Gregory Endowed Chair. *Each Knuckle with Sugar* won the *Driftwood Press* Open Reading Contest and is her debut collection.

MORE TITLES FROM
DRIFTWOOD PRESS

comics, fiction, poetry
chapbooks & collections

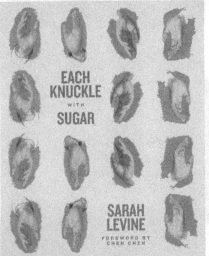

Printed in the USA
CPSIA information can be obtained
at www.ICGtesting.com
JSHW051930281223
54440JS00002B/6